Personal Testimonies by Those Impacted by

A Light Shines Bright in Babylon

"Buck Jacobs is himself a shining light in the Babylon of business. He brings years of real world experience running businesses and applying Scripture to leadership and decision-making in the marketplace. This book is a gem for Christian business owners."

Dr. David W. Miller, Executive Director
Yale University Center for Faith & Culture

"Enlightening, challenging and convicting – the most concise book on "pursuing performance God's way" I've ever read, enabling me to see how to develop a business based on building strong vibrant relationships with God and man. Well done, Buck!"

Wally Armstrong, PGA Tour Veteran
Teacher & Author

"A convicting work that reveals God's plan to share the love of Jesus everyday, at work, in the marketplace. After you read this, any notion that church ends Sunday morning will be transformed into seeing a whole new mission field."

David L. Dunkel, Chairman & CEO
KForce, Inc. (Nasdaq: KFRC)

"Of all the books on Faith & Business, Buck Jacobs' LSB is unique in combining a sound Biblical foundation with a gripping personal call to life-changing commitment to Christ the person, rather than to Christian principles. He offers the serious Christian business owner a blueprint for a business life that will produce eternal fruit."

John E. Mulford, PhD, Director
Regent University Center for Entrepreneurship

"This book changed my entire focus in leading a business and is a must read for any CEO desiring God's perspective. I've given copies to several business owner friends."

Peter Lane, Owner & President
Ivey Lane Inc.

"No one in the workplace ministry movement has had so great an impact on so many lives as Buck Jacobs. He is truly a patriarch for the cause. Please join me and many thousands of other CEOs who are captivated by this great book."

Mark Cress, President/CEO
Corporate Chaplains of America

"This book explains clearly the Biblical basis for the growing marketplace ministry movement among Christians and shows each of us how we can have eternal results from our jobs, regardless of our position or title."

Steve Wilson, President
Hide-Away Storage Services Inc.

"I've recommended this book to hundreds because it expresses a truth that most churches and seminaries don't fully appreciate. Business people can be in 'full-time ministry' better than clergy because they are able to not only speak the message but demonstrate it through the way they do business, the way they treat people, and the way they handle money. This book is for business people who get tempted to go to seminary. Hopefully it will keep many Spirit-filled leaders in the marketplace where they belong."

Judge Tim Philpot, Former President
CBMC International

A LIGHT SHINES BRIGHT IN BABYLON

Buck Jacobs

A HANDBOOK FOR
CHRISTIAN BUSINESS OWNERS

A Light Shines Bright in Babylon
By Buck Jacobs
Copyright ©1992, 2005, 2007

ISBN 0-9786039-1-5
For Worldwide Distribution
Printed in the U.S.A.

Lanphier Press
U.S.A.
www.lanphierpress.com

The C12 Group, LLC
U.S.A.
www.c12group.com

From the Author

For more than 25 years, I have been gripped by a vision and challenged by the Word of the Lord through Habakkuk. In the vision, which is constantly before me, I am standing on a hill overlooking a vast city. The city is cloaked in darkness, but there are glowing lights piercing that dark veil. In fact, there are many lights and the area around some of these points of light have actually been brightened. The darkness is actually being pushed back here and there.

The city represents the marketplace. It is dark with sin and sick with greed and lust. The marketplace has been called a jungle but I think it is worse than a jungle. For sure, it's Babylon, which the Bible presents as the symbol of all that is wrong with the world.

The lights are companies in the marketplace that are different. Oh, they do many of the same kinds of things that the other companies do, but in very different ways. They are companies run by people who belong to Christ and it is because they serve an all-powerful, loving God that these business owners do things differently. It is through these differences that The Light shines. The greater the difference, the brighter the light. The city will become brighter and brighter and the darkness will flee as Christians let His light shine in their niche of the marketplace.

This is my vision for each one of you.

"THE WORD" ON BUSINESS

"No other foundation can anyone lay than that which is laid,
which is Jesus Christ."
1 Corinthians 3:11

"For everyone to whom much is given, from him much will be required;
and to whom much has been committed, of him they will ask the more."
Luke 12:48b

"For we must all appear before the judgment seat of Christ,
that each one may receive the things done in the body,
according to what he had done, whether good or bad."
2 Corinthians 5:10

"Now if anyone builds on this foundation with gold, silver, precious
stones, wood, hay, straw, each one's work will become clear;
for the Day will declare it, because it will be revealed by fire;
and the fire will test each one's work, of what sort it is. If anyone's
work which he has built on it endures, he will receive a reward.
If anyone's work is burned, he will suffer loss;
but he himself will be saved, yet so as through fire."
1 Corinthians 3:12-15

"Do not lay up for yourself treasures on earth, where moth and rust
destroys and where thieves break in and steal; but lay up for yourselves
treasures in heaven, where neither moth or rust destroys
and where thieves do not break in and steal.
For where your treasure is, there your heart will be also."
Matthew 6:19-21

"No one can serve two masters; for either he will hate the one and
love the other, or else he will be loyal to one and despise the other.
You cannot serve God and mammon."
Matthew 6:24

"And I say to you, make friends for yourselves by unrighteous mammon,
that when you fail they may receive you into an everlasting home.
He who is faithful in what is least is faithful also in much;
and he who is unjust in what is least is unjust also in much.
Therefore if you have not been faithful in the unrighteous mammon,
who will commit to your trust the true riches? And if you have not been
faithful in what is another man's who will give you what is your own?"
Luke 16:9-12

"Seek first the kingdom of God and His righteousness,
and all these things shall be added to you."
Matthew 6:33

"My kingdom is not of this world."
John 18:36a

TABLE OF CONTENTS

YOU HAVE A HOLY CALLING

God's primary purpose is always the same, regardless of what area He may choose to operate in. The methods and arena of operation are very different, but His purpose never changes. Your company is not a church but its purpose is ultimately the same as that of the church. It is your ministry. Your business is your platform for ministry, uniquely given to you by God to run for Him, to use for His glory and the building up and equipping of His Body.

If you are called by God to run His company, your calling is as holy as that of any pastor, priest or missionary. The person placed in charge of a property belonging to the Most High God is a person given a sacred task.

If you are given a company to run for God it is the leading ministry opportunity in your life. It is the primary area of Kingdom service outside of your personal worship and relationship with God and your ministry to your family. It is not just one of several, it is the primary and, in most cases, the only additional ministry that God has specifically given to you. Many spend their lives entangled in ministry efforts that could and should be done by others, thereby squandering the one ministry opportunity that only they can fulfill. Leading your company for God cannot be delegated. It's you or no one. Others can follow, but, in this instance, you must lead.

The consequences of you understanding this truth are eternal. Fulfilling God's purposes through our lives, and properly using the tools He places in our hands to do so, are the crux of the Christian life after conversion and prior to going on to being with Him in heaven. No Christian wants to hear, "Why do you call me Lord, Lord, and do not do the things I say?" (Luke 6:46).

We do not want to hear it now, but it would be far worse to hear it later, after this life is over. The things we do with our businesses, and how we do them, are relevant to this equation. We cannot afford blind spots. We need clear vision.

A Light Shines Bright in Babylon

Chapter 1

THE TRUE "ROLLOVER"

> Then he said to them, "Watch out! Be on your guard against all kinds of greed; a man's life does not consist in the abundance of his possessions."
>
> And he told them this parable: "The ground of a certain rich man produced a good crop. He thought to himself, 'What shall I do? I have no place to store my crops.'
>
> "Then he said, 'This is what I'll do. I will tear down my barns and build bigger ones, and there I will store all my grain and my goods. And I'll say to myself, "You have plenty of good things laid up for many years. Take life easy; eat, drink and be merry." '
>
> "But God said to him, 'You fool! This very night your life will be demanded from you. Then who will get what you have prepared for yourself?'
>
> "This is how it will be with anyone who stores up things for himself but is not rich toward God."
>
> Luke 12:15-21 (NIV)

What would you do if your most trusted and proven financial advisor were to come to you tomorrow and say: "I have some information that you really need. It is absolutely certain and without doubt that as of a certain date, which is not known, but certain to come, and could be very soon, the dollar is going to be declared worthless and will be replaced with seashells as the medium of exchange. I stake my life on the certain truth of what I have told you."

What would be your first thought if someone told you seashells would be the next form of money? Most people, when confronted with this "let's suppose" scenario, answer something like this: "I would immediately begin to figure out ways to exchange my dollars for seashells."

They would do a "rollover", exchanging one asset for a more attractive one. And who wouldn't, really? If this advisor had real credibility and there were a way to exchange dollars for seashells, any such effort would be worthwhile. Obviously, there would be a very powerful motivation to exchange something doomed to become worthless for something that will replace it in enduring value.

The seashells metaphor may be stretching things a bit, but the part about the dollar being declared valueless is guaranteed to happen for each of us. Dollars will be absolutely, without doubt, valueless the moment we take our last breath. From that point on, there will be a new "coin of the realm," and dollars will have nothing to do with it. Every dollar we have left when we draw our last breath will be lost to our benefit forever. We can't reach back from the grave and snatch some dollars to take along. Dollars will not be needed.

However, if we hurry, we can exchange, or "rollover," our dollars for the future "coin of the realm". Jesus promises us in the Sermon on the Mount that we can store up "treasure in heaven where moth and rust do not destroy, and thieves do not break in to steal."

What is the coin of heaven? What has value up there? These are simple questions with a simple answer: people. Only people will have value in heaven. We can exchange our earthly dollars for heavenly treasure by investing them in the process of the salvation and sanctification of people and in service to the people God loves.

We can use our dollars either for earthly purposes or we can exchange our dollars now for things of eternal value. There is no doubt the day will come when our dollars will be worthless to us. No man avoids it, and that day almost always comes sooner than expected. And once the day comes, it is final, and no more exchanges or "rollovers" are possible. But until that day there are great opportunities for massively profitable "rollovers" to eternal values.

Dollars are only one of the tools God gives us to exchange. The other "tools for exchange" that we have are our talents, abilities, time, gifts, education, experience, position and reputation. They all have value only here, but that sort of "value" will not count for much in heaven.

A truly wise business person always looks for the greatest return on his or her investment. No shrewd investor wants to get caught holding a worthless position. Even investments that have been profitable for a long period must be liquidated and reinvested when we see that their usefulness is ending.

Think deeply about this metaphor. It's not a matter of whether or not it is true for you and me. It is absolutely true. The only question before us is the date of exchange.

Converting your dollars in your company into seashells is your decision. If you are the owner no one can make that particular decision for you. In your business you are the number one decision maker, whatever your title. If you own a company, whether it has thousands of employees or only yourself, you are in a unique position. No one else in the world can do what God asks you to do in your company. You establish policy, you determine the "corporate culture," and the buck stops with you.

Your business is your primary platform for ministry which God has given to you alone. No one else can do what you can as it relates to your firm. God has given you a company to run for Him and to use for the building up and equipping of His Body. The products you make or services you supply are only a vehicle, a means to an end. The end is service to the King!

Satan tries terribly hard to make us deny this truth and believe that dollars are far more important then seashells. In reality, however, dollars have no value in the Kingdom of God except as they are converted or relate to producing "seashells".

We are talking about "hardball Christianity." It may not be the kind of Christianity you see every day, but it is the kind of Christianity that will change the world! It is simply being consistent in our daily lives with what Jesus clearly taught. It is normal Biblical Christianity. Jesus didn't come to improve the world. He came to radically change it. He promised that they who follow Him would do the same things He did and even greater (John 14:12).

But you must be willing to play "hardball Christianity." You can touch hundreds of lives, maybe even thousands or tens of thousands through your role as head of your firm. You actually can do more than all but the very largest churches, but you have got to believe the "seashells" are what is really important. You have to develop what is called an "eternal perspective."

Jesus clearly had that eternal perspective. This is expressed so vividly by the writer of Hebrews, declaring that Christ, "who for the joy that was set before Him endured the cross, despising the shame, and has sat down at the right hand of the throne of God" (Hebrews 12:2b).

Jesus is our example in all things. He clearly lived on earth with Heaven on His mind. We can too! People who live like that are different. Not better merely by degree, but *very* different. Let me repeat that again: not better by degree, but very different. They are not average, but exceptional. They stand out from the crowd. They make an impact on those around them. How about you? Can you play "hardball Christianity"? Let's look at some of the rules.

Chapter 2

CONCEPTS OF
A COMPANY FOR CHRIST

The statement is so, so simple:

> *"All that I have is a gift from God,*
> *and I am only a manager or steward of it."*

It is amazing what profound implications can come out of such a simple statement. Let's look at four basic concepts that inevitably flow from that declaration. Then we will examine the two reasons that most Christians who own or run companies give lip service to this simple Biblical truth, but do not really practice it.

Here are some basic principles which each Christian business owner or operator needs to understand:

Principle #1:

We Cannot "Divide" Our Lives

Sin is sin no matter where you are or what you are doing. Your actions at work are not overlooked, no matter how much money you are giving to the church. There is no special exception that allows Christians to do things in business that they could not do in church.

Lying, cheating, taking unfair advantage, uncaring acts, unloving behavior, using or abusing people or any other sinful act or attitude are just as unacceptable to Jesus at work as they are at home, in church or anywhere else. The ends never justify the means. The means establish the value and quality of the end.

If just this first principle, that we cannot "divide" our lives, were put into practice, the face of the marketplace and the testimony of Christian business leaders would be radically different.

Christ is Lord of all or He is not Lord at all! Very few understand such a simple logical extension of basic truth. Jesus told us clearly that we "cannot serve two masters." He didn't say that it would be hard or difficult or dangerous. He said, "Cannot." Impossible. No way! If Jesus ever gave an unequivocal teaching, here it is: "No one can serve two masters; for either he will hate the one and love the other, or else he will be loyal to one and despise the other. You cannot serve God and mammon" (Matthew 6:24).

Principle #2:

YOU Don't Own It!

Your business does not belong to you but to God. You are merely a steward or manager of it. The day will come when you will be called to account for your performance in that position. Don't be deceived. God never looks the other way. Never. Sixty seconds of every minute, twenty-four hours of every day, you are responsible to God for what He has given you to care for.

If you are having a hard time with this statement, I challenge you to prove for yourself, once and for all, whether it is true or not. The test is very simple. Just pray this prayer: "Dear God, I don't believe that you own my business. I created it, I worked to build it and it's mine. So God, in order to settle this issue of ownership once and for all, I challenge You to take away all of my business that is Yours and leave me what is mine."

When put in these terms I have yet to meet a sincere Christian who would take the challenge and pray the prayer. Yet so few really walk in this truth that God owns their business.

Principle #3:

God's Standard is NOT the World's!

The standards that will apply to Jesus Christ's judgment of your performance in the role of His steward will be radically different from those applied by the world. Worldly standards of success, wealth, reputation, and status WILL NOT be those Jesus uses. He never has and He never will. God's standard for His stewards is a fruitful life rooted in obedience and faithfulness to the opportunity of participating in building the Kingdom of God. Read that sentence again in light of the Parable of the Talents in Matthew 25.

How well you and I use the opportunities that God presents us to share in His work will produce rewards. If we do not use the opportunities, we will suffer loss at our promised judgment or accounting. You see, in reality your business is simply a platform from which you may choose to serve the Lord. It has many functions, but only one major purpose (see 2 Corinthians 3:11-15 and John 15:1-8).

Look at it this way: if you were the manager of a company that was owned by another person, you would be obligated to operate based on the owner's standards and values. None of us would disagree with that idea. So, what's so difficult with the concept of operating a business according to God's standard, since He owns the business?

The functions that make up your business, such as producing products, services, and profits, have only temporary value. Their eternal purpose is to serve God by providing a vehicle that facilitates participating in His work and producing eternal fruit.

What is really most important to you: that which seems good for now or that which is great forever? The difference in value between what is temporal and what is eternal is immense...immeasurable in fact!

Principle #4:

Your Business IS Your Ministry!

Because of the sheer amount of dedicated time involved, your opportunity for Kingdom service is greatest while you are at work. Hence your responsibility before God is greatest here and is highly impacted by how you see your business and what you do with it as you participate in producing eternal fruit.

Does it make any sense that God would call you to serve Him and promise to reward obedience in service, but somehow deny you the opportunity to participate in the very area of life where you spend the majority of your time?

Nonsense! Quite the contrary. Rather than deny you the opportunity to participate, God requires it, and holds you responsible for your performance in relation to it. "To whom much has been committed, of him they will ask the more" (Luke 12:48b).

If these principles are true, then why are they unclear to so many and followed by so few?

One reason is that many people have never been taught these principles as they relate to the business world. Most Christians can go to church all their lives and never hear more than a handful of sermons relating to business practices. The marketplace where we spend most of our time is largely neglected. If we happen to be Christians who own and operate businesses, there is even less applicable teaching or understanding available.

Business owners are typically looked upon as good prospects to serve on administering boards and as potentially generous givers. But precious little attention has been given to their special needs and problems. The purpose given most often for their being in business is to "make money to fund Christian ministries and causes."

Another reason so few Christians practice "stewardship," rather than "ownership," of their business is the deception that is in this world. We have an enemy who has deceived us. He is also God's enemy and His name is Satan. He is the ruler of this world, and Babylon is his system. It is totally unlike the kingdom of God. His system has totally different values because it is a kingdom of "this world only."

Everything in Satan's kingdom is short-term, relating only to this temporal life. God's kingdom includes this life, yes, but more importantly by far, the life yet to come - eternal life. Satan is judged already. He is not eternal. Christians are eternal, here and hereafter.

Satan sets up all kinds of shiny distractions and deceptive attractions, but they are all flawed. They don't ever satisfy or live up to their promise and they are all of value in this life only. If we get sucked into the adversary's value system, we can spend our whole lives succeeding here only to fail forever. We can generate tremendous worldly success only to be found to be eternally bankrupt. We can end our lives experiencing the good, while missing the best.

Chapter 3

PROFITS:
NEW LIGHT ON AN OLD TOPIC

Profits seem to me to be a nearly neglected topic in Christian teaching. Over the years I have found very little written and heard very little discussion concerning God's perspective on profits. I have heard lots of people telling me what I need to do with profits, if I have them. There has been much appropriate-sounding advice, but very little thought, about the purpose of profits and how they fit into the overall picture of a company run for Christ.

Many have mistakenly thought that once an owner realizes that his business really belongs to God, and dedicates it to Him, it will automatically become very profitable. They are very often disappointed. These false expectations are built in a faulty understanding of the Bible and lead to disappointment and discouragement. Many simply give up at this point. It is sad when this happens because of a lack of understanding as to the real nature and purpose of God in providing for profit in our business.

Let's begin by defining profits, looking at their source, and then consider how they should be used. We can define profits as what is left over after we pay all the expenses of doing business. Don't get hung up about whether they are gross or net, based on depreciation or whatever. Let's keep it simple: profits are what we take in over what we spend.

There are only two sources of profits. I'm sure many of you will quickly agree that God is the source of profits. But will you also agree that Satan can be a source of profits? Many do not realize that Satan can bring profits, since God has delegated him to be the "prince of this world." Satan told Jesus that all the kingdoms of this earth and their glory had been given to him and that he could dish out whatever he wanted to whomever he chose (Luke 4:5-6). If your heart can be bought with money, Satan can and will meet your price. Peace, however, is another story!

The Source of Profits

It can be confusing, with both Satan and God capable of providing profits. But there are two surefire tests that we can use to determine whether the source of our profits is God or Satan. These tests only work if we are willing to be honest:

1. Whose values are being promoted - God's or Satan's?

If the profits promote the things that God has pointed out to be priorities in your life, then the profits are from God. Satan does not promote God's values. God promotes God's values.

God always has His finger on something in our lives that He is trying to develop, something that He is trying to promote, change, remove or instill. Many times it is for us to spend more time with Him, first in our day. This may be time in the study of His Word, time in prayer, time listening to Him, or just plain quiet time. The highest priority in our lives should be knowing Him. Our growth involves knowing Him better and having a deepening relationship with Him. All else of value in our lives flows out from our relationship with God.

At other times He may be working on personal relationships in our lives, or humility, trust or faith. Normally we know where God is working in our lives if we are honest with ourselves. If your company's profits allow you to develop whatever it is that God has shown you to be important, then the profits are from Him.

2. What price do you have to pay for profits?

On the other hand, if the price of increased profits is that you have less time for God, or relationships deteriorate, or Bible study is squeezed out, then the profits are not from God. God is consistent, and He never plays games with His revealed priorities. He never sacrifices a marriage to build a business or sacrifices a sacred priority to build something of temporal value.

The stereotypical 'driven' CEO, who works 80-100 hours a week, is a stranger to his family, a ghost in church, and has no time for recreation, relaxation or reflection is a satanic cultural reality. But this is not a Biblical model for leadership.

So it really is not too hard to discern the source of profits. The hard part is being honest with ourselves.

The Use of Profits

Let's assume that our profits are God's profits. What would be some of the legitimate purposes of His profits? I have often asked Christian CEO's, Owners and Presidents this question, and the most common answers are:

- Grow the company
- Promote the sharing of the Gospel
- Meet the needs of people
- Savings for a "rainy day"
- Fund God's work through various ministries
- Added research and development to improve quality

It is extremely interesting that I have never heard anyone say, "to provide the owner with an extravagant lifestyle," or "to buy more things for the CEO," or "to enable the President to enjoy a personal standard of living far above anyone else in the company."

Yet the truth is, and *everyone* knows it, that those things are what most often happen when a business prospers. As profits build, the CEO's personal income (and all that goes with it) increases much faster than anyone else's. This is as true in the companies owned by Christians as non-Christians. All of a sudden there are new cars, bigger homes, and more expensive toys and trips. It would be nice if there also were more peace, joy, love and more time to enjoy God, our family and things of real importance. But that is seldom the case.

But is it necessarily wrong to enjoy a better lifestyle due to the fruit of our labors? Is wealth bad? No! It is not wrong in itself to have more things or to be wealthy. But what *is* wrong is to do so without God's permission. The error comes in not asking this question:

> *"God, here is the increase from your company,*
> *how do You want me to use it?"*

Very few Christian business leaders bother to ask that question. Why do you suppose they don't ask? Maybe they don't want to risk hearing the answer!

You cannot assume that because you are the one that He used to produce the profit that God wants you to consume or hoard it all. If they are His profits, then He should decide how to use them. God may want you to have the profits to elevate your lifestyle. But if He does, it will only be to use you to build His kingdom in a different place or socioeconomic strata.

God places His people in every strata of society, from bottom to top. And it is very hard to realize that He is the one who calls each to their strata. The top stratum lives a very different lifestyle from the bottom, but their purpose from God's perspective is the same.

The purpose for which some Christians are given and entrusted with much is NOT so that they may simply enjoy the limited pleasures of this world. The purpose is to glorify Him and to promote His kingdom. If God gives profits, it is to promote His kingdom. If He gives poverty, it also is to promote His kingdom. Neither poverty nor riches in themselves glorify God. A rich Christian brings no more glory to God than a poor one. God is not glorified in what we have, but in who we are. The mystery of the gospel is Christ in us, not gold on us!

God will support any company that will use the profits to promote His kingdom. The reason why many companies owned by Christians are not profitable is because their owners would misunderstand the purpose of the profits.

Why Profits are Withheld

He may have to withhold profits to get our attention in one way or another. As Walter Meloon, the godly chairman of Correct Craft Corporation has declared, "God doesn't give us lots of things because He can't trust us with them."

A few reasons God might withhold profits include:

- We might only squander the profits on ourselves and suffer eternal loss (1 Corinthians 3:11-15)
- We would use the profits to gain power over others that He does not want us to have
- They might hinder basic character development that God wants to see in us

God may not have called us to the business in the first place, and profits would encourage us down a path He does not want us to take. Think about this one! Have you ever really asked the question,

"God, where do you want me to serve you? In this business or somewhere else?"

The true purpose of profits in a company God owns is to promote God's kingdom. You can be sure that God is providing the profits when your life is in order with God first, family next, then ministry, and finally work. Such profits will:

- Promote salvation of souls
- Encourage believers toward godly discipline
- Contribute to acts of love and charity for those in need

At times it is very difficult for us to be objective both about the use of profits and our attitudes toward them, when we have profits. It also is hard for us, in different ways, when profits are absent. Both in feast and in famine, the counsel of wise advisors can be a wonderful help. A group of like-minded, spiritually mature people who will pray *for* us and *with* us, provide trustworthy counsel, and help us hear from God is a priceless asset.

Chapter 4

SURROUNDED!
BY OPPORTUNITIES

General Custer, in the hours before his last battle, was surrounded by thousands and didn't know it. Like Custer, many business owners and leaders cannot see the large and immensely hungry mission throng that is all around them.

These Christian business leaders often send money to overseas missionaries, which is good, and they may give time to their church outreach programs, which also is good. They may support para church ministries of various kinds. But they are blinded to a huge personal ministry opportunity with a group of persons with whom they have a direct relationship which provides them a unique opportunity to lead, evangelize, disciple and touch for Christ.

Who makes up this great "unnoticed" mass? It is our employees, our customers, our suppliers, our trade associates and our competitors. They are our marketplace mission field. They are a normal and natural part of each of our businesses. We already have relationships with them. We don't need to look any further for an incredibly fruitful mission field.

We deal with this huge mission field constantly. They are there every day, every month, each year. We encourage them, motivate them, solicit them, correct them, seek them, influence them, hire them, fire them, negotiate with them, placate them, buy from them, sell to them and so on. Our lives are truly interwoven with theirs!

Even the smallest business is likely to have 250 persons or more with whom it has contact in a year. Most modest businesses touch thousands! If you think I am exaggerating, try this test. Get out a pencil and paper and start adding these numbers:

- How many **employees** do you have? Write the number down. Do you have contact with their families? Could you have contact with their families if you wanted to? If so, add again that number.

- How many people knock on your door looking for work each year? Add this number of **applicants** or inquirers to your list.

- How many **suppliers** do you deal with? Include those you use as well as those who solicit your business.

- How many **customers** will you have contact with this year? Include those who buy, those you call on but don't buy, and those who merely inquire. What about those who see your trade advertising or receive routine marketing materials?

- How many other **trade association** friends and competitors do you interact with in a year? Include those who are in your market area and also those who are outside your market. Don't forget those whom you come into contact with in the Chamber of Commerce, as well as networking and community benevolence organizations.

Add all the totals together. This grand total gives you a rough estimate of the size of the mission field that you are responsible for. Think about it. How many churches touch more lives than your company? Over the years, in estimating the size of this mission field with hundreds of small to mid-sized companies, we have seen a typical estimate in the 5,000-10,000 range.

How many testimonies of well-known missionaries have you heard who have dedicated their entire lives to reach a fraction of that number in some far off jungle? We honor and revere them for their commitment, as we should, but we also need to realize that the "harvest is white" right around our own business.

Every business has built within its natural function perhaps the greatest opportunity to give our testimony to the Gospel that we will ever have. This is because it is so unusual to find Christ in the marketplace. Most people expect to be exploited or manipulated by others in the marketplace. The rules by which the world plays are rough and self-serving. When the love of God is encountered in this darkness, it shines even brighter.

Do you realize that each soul that your company touches is just as precious to God as any in the most far away jungle? Each lost person who passes your way in the course of doing business of one kind or another is one that your Savior died for just as certainly as He did for you!

In every relationship there exists the potential to share the Gospel

20

in some manner. Some opportunities are very brief and limited, some very personal and intense. But, in each relational contact, the potential exists.

So what can you do? Where do you go from here?

First, recognize that your business is a vehicle that you can use to reach out and share the love of Christ in many different ways.

Second, take the time to identify and understand the make up of your marketplace mission field. In other words, spend some time putting your finger on the many people who in one way or another come in contact with your firm during the course of a year.

Third, ask God to open your eyes to the opportunity that He has given you and lead you into creative ways to exploit it.

Fourth, seek out other like-minded men and women to share fellowship with, learn from, and to whom you can be accountable.

Fifth, begin to minister as God leads you. Do at least one thing, little or big, to start. Encourage your like-minded staff to join in.

Don't be discouraged if your pastor, Christian friends, or other Christian business owners don't understand you. If they all did understand this book would not be necessary.

Let me mention another point worth considering. Whether we like it or not, we are sharing about Christ and His priority in our lives, whether we mean to or not. I can illustrate what I mean from my own experience. Shortly after I became a Christian, I saw a pamphlet in a book rack at church with the title "What Religion Are You Teaching Your Children?" The very first sentence of that book said, in effect, "Even if you are teaching no religion to your children you are teaching them that no religion is important."

I realized that my life, my actions, and what I actually did portrayed my true self, including my religion, to my child. This was in spite of the fact that I had never even tried to talk with her about religion!

If our testimony is real and good, those with whom we relate through the business will be influenced toward God. If it is false and shallow, they may be turned from Him. If your company is saying nothing about Christ, then isn't it reasonable to assume that those you make contact with through the business will subconsciously conclude that you do not think that Christ is important in the marketplace?

Let's change the title of that little pamphlet I saw at church to say:

> **WHAT IS YOUR COMPANY SAYING ABOUT JESUS CHRIST TO YOUR EMPLOYEES, CUSTOMERS, SUPPLIERS AND OTHERS?**

The truth is we are always sharing the Gospel - as we really understand it or believe it - as we relate to other people. We share it by what we say, what we do, and who we are. We share it by displaying our values through our actions over time. Our demonstrated values are really our testimony. We give it in hundreds and thousands of ways, every minute of every day.

Here are two suggestions to help you:

- *Look to the Lord.* Decide that you will spend more time with Him and then do it. Maybe the answer for you is to get to work fifteen minutes earlier and spend the time in Bible study with the request, "God show me in your Word how to deal with the things I will have to decide on and face today in such a way that Your love and the truth of Your Word will shine through my actions. Run Your company through me today."

- *Expect miracles and opposition.* Your life very well may be transformed as your perspective changes from temporal to eternal in decision-making and evaluating each situation. Your business may take on a significance to you that it has never had before. The knowledge that we are working for something far greater than immediate profits has a wonderful effect.

In my own life, the awareness that I was serving Jesus in the process of all my business dealings allowed me to function joyfully and successfully for over 10 years in a business that I basically disliked. The business was a specialty chemical business. I am not a chemist and had no formal training in applied chemistry. I was frustrated by my lack of knowledge and inability to provide immediate answers much of the time, but the realization that each day brought me the chance to participate in God's great work was fulfilling and exciting. This satisfaction far exceeded the excitement of doing deals and making money. It survives to this day.

Chapter 5

BLIND SPOTS
& OTHER HANDICAPS

Our ability to minister in and through our businesses rests on three distinct "legs." Like the old fashioned three-legged stool, if any one of the legs is weak, the whole platform will be shaky. The stronger and steadier the platform, the better chance for the long-term success of the ministry.

Each of us needs to understand that, whether we realize it or not, all that we do is constantly being watched by those we relate to in business. Everything we do, especially as we reach out to minister, is being held up to the standard of what they perceive Christian actions should be. Most of those watching us may not really understand the Gospel deeply, but they know that Jesus wouldn't lie or cheat or hurt people. They have all heard the Golden Rule.

Let's look at each of these three legs to see how they affect our ability to share God's love in the marketplace.

Leg #1:

How We Deal with People

Our business is nothing more than a collection of people dealing with other people, so how **we** personally deal with people and view people is tremendously important.

If we treat people with contempt or indifference, how likely are they to listen to us when we tell them of God's love and its effect on our lives?

If we cheat on our taxes, how likely is our verbal testimony to be received by our unbelieving CPA?

If we use people to our advantage and their expense, how willing do you suppose they and those others watching will be when we ask them to visit our church?

If we don't keep our word in little things, how credible will we be when we tell people about Jesus?

In short, if we treat them just like the world treats them, are they likely to hear us? Should they?

On the other hand, if we can learn to see each person through Jesus' eyes, don't you think that over time they might want to listen? We need to filter all of our actions regarding people through His perspective, and live our lives by constantly asking, "What would Jesus do?" This is certainly not easy, given the conditioning most of us have experienced through the years and the business advice we have picked up along the way. We really do not have any better choice than to constantly ask ourselves, "What would Jesus do?" and try to treat them as He would

History shows us that people admire and respect others who truly stand for something, but they have deep contempt for hypocrites who say one thing and do another. Jesus called hypocrisy "the leaven of the Pharisees." In this age of "spin" and politically correct lingo, it is still infecting us.

The times when our attitude toward others is most obviously revealed is when we are under pressure. When there are disagreements and conflicts we are more likely to "blow it." This is especially true when money is involved or when we feel mistreated or angry. That's when we are mostly likely to demonstrate that things, money or our ego are more important than other people. Jesus would not see it that way!

How do we guard against these all too "natural" reactions? The answer is to constantly have before us the question "What would Jesus do?" This is, of course, truly possible only when we have intimacy with Him through the study of His Word and prayer.

Some say genuine Christianity is best demonstrated during conflict. I say it's ONLY demonstrated during conflict. We're not tested in agreement, but in disagreement.

Our relationships are the practical demonstration of the faith that is in us. If our lives at home or work or church are filled with broken, contentious, unloving relationships, then something is drastically wrong. If the way we treat people through business is a hindrance or stumbling block to their seeing Christ in us, we are missing the boat!

Leg #2:

How We Deal with Money

Our platform for ministry will never be strong if we are "money hungry." We can hide it at church, and maybe even fool some of our friends. But in the business world, we cannot hide it if we love money more than people and serve money rather than human needs.

Let me be very clear that I am NOT saying that diligence, making a profit, and being prudent with money are unimportant. We must be good stewards. We are commanded to be diligent and wise stewards. Money *is* important. But money is NOT MORE important than people or God's principles.

If we value profit over people, others will certainly know it. Our actions will speak louder than anything we can say. If we pursue dollars with greater zeal than the Kingdom of God, everyone will ultimately realize it. If we are willing to violate God's principles to grow or maintain our business, the hypocrisy will show sooner rather than later.

Jesus used money to serve people, He never used people to serve money. We need to have the same mind-set toward money that characterized Jesus. We need to see money as simply a tool to bring forward the love of God in various ways. If we have this attitude toward money, it will show and we will be in a position to have a powerful ministry.

Our attitude toward money is watched constantly within our marketplace mission field. How we handle it will have a major influence on how we are received when we attempt to testify or show Christ or give a credible account for the faith that we have.

Leg #3:

How We Deal with the Integrity and Quality of Our Products and Services

This third leg of our platform for ministry can be a real blind spot, especially for some people who may not have a major problem in dealing with people or money. This leg for ministry involves our integrity and the quality of our work. Haven't we all heard countless horror stories about Christians having business dealings with other

Christians and coming away disappointed and regretful? That's not the way it should be. We should look forward to business dealings with other professing Christians. Unfortunately, all too often we dread it because many Christian business leaders do not understand the importance of the integrity and the quality of their products and services.

We should have a commitment to quality and integrity which is second to none. Our minimum goal should be serving the customer to the very best of our ability and doing our work "as to the Lord" (Colossians 3:23-24).

This does not mean that every Christian in business will always be the best in his or her area of expertise at a given time. But it does mean that they will be committed to being the best at what God has asked them to do with the resources God has provided. God will fully develop the talents and abilities that He has placed within us if we will allow Him and trust Him. We should commit ourselves to be all we can for Him and to use all He gives us for the eternal benefit of others.

What can you do to strengthen these three legs of your platform for ministry? You can:

- Ask God to show you areas of weakness in any of the three legs. Be open enough to let God identify the areas where you are weakest and commit yourself to work to improve those areas.

- Convene a council of advisors or join a local C12 Group and ask others who will be honest with you to help.

- Ask your employees to rate you and your company in each area. Survey your customers and suppliers. Ask them to tell you honestly how you rate in key areas of your relationship.

- Ask your closest friend if he or she thinks you care more about things and money or people and serving the Lord.

Small amounts of consistent effort over a long period of time will yield very large results.

Chapters eight through ten are devoted to helping you work toward enhancing each leg of your business ministry platform.

Chapter 6

EIGHT BASIC PRACTICES
OF A CHRISTIAN COMPANY

In all areas of life, it is the basics that count. Our long-term success in marketplace ministry will pretty much depend upon our practicing and mastering a handful of basics. Look over the following contributing characteristics of a company for Christ and see how they relate to you and your three legs of ministry. Where you find the greatest weaknesses in your practice, make a commitment to improve in these areas right away!

Companies dedicated to carrying Christ's message actively into the marketplace generally will have:

1 *Respect for, reverence for, and submission to the authority of God's written Word and its fundamental principles*

In a company for Christ, no known violations of Biblical principle will be tolerated in policy or practice. Where such violation or deviation is found, plans for immediate correction are implemented. No company will ever be successful in marketplace ministry while consistently violating known Biblical truth.

God's Word is honored, perhaps even displayed, maybe incorporated into company literature and, when appropriate, referred to in real day-to-day situations. All this must be done in good taste and according to the gifts and personality of the person responsible to lead in the business (CEO, President, etc.). One outcome of this will be the practice of sound stewardship and Biblical attitudes toward money and people.

The Bible must have real authority!

2 *The practice of prayer is openly acknowledged and demonstrated to be an integral part of the business*

Prayer is utilized before decisions are made and is consistently offered for employees, customers, suppliers and associates of the company for Christ. When possible, the practice of prayer is acknowledged to those being prayed for. I have never had anyone say "no thanks" to my offer to pray for them in a time of trouble or need.

God's guidance through prayer is valued, sought and depended upon. There may, if appropriate, be a company prayer meeting, perhaps even on company time. Prayer needs and answers might be recognized in a newsletter, web-based bulletin board or logbook. Employees will grow to see the value of prayer in the life and decisions of their leader.

Our company eventually had three separate prayer times: one for the office, one for the lab, and one for the factory. These times were staggered so that business was not interrupted. They were held first thing in the morning. Over the years these times were the source of many wonderful experiences for all of us. Attendance was always voluntary and not everyone always came. Over the span of a decade it served as an immensely profitable time and added tremendously to our experience, growth, and team culture.

❸ *A heart for evangelism*

Any company that stands for Christ must have a heart for the lost, although that does not mean that each company will be active in direct evangelism. But the firm's leader(s) will have a sincere desire to see the lost saved. They will know that Jesus died so that people could and would be saved. Nothing is more important to God than his children being saved. It's the only thing He gave His Son to die for. Jesus did not die so that our marriages could be strengthened, to meet our financial needs, or to heal our physical ills. He does bless our marriages, provide finances and heal our bodies. But that's not why He had to die. He had to die so we could be saved and reconciled to God the Father for eternity.

The activities of our companies, if they are truly committed to ministry in the marketplace, will support the work of evangelism in various ways.

❹ *A clear and concise statement of its purpose*

The purpose of the company should be reduced to one or two sentences that reflect the clear articulation of the owner's vision for the business. This statement should be easily committed to memory so that it can be brought readily to mind in the heat of the moment.

The statement of purpose (also known as a mission statement) should be used as the final arbiter for decision-making at all levels of the company. Any action or strategy which is clearly counter to our stated purpose can be discarded out of hand. Anything that is not clear must be tested further and perhaps refined or modified. Those actions or strategies that clearly support the mission can be implemented without fear. A proper statement of purpose is a tremendous help in keeping the company focused and properly directed.[1]

A willingness to give from the increase of the business to support the Lord's work

It's God's business. A legitimate function of a business yielded to Christ is to fund Christian work both within internally and externally.[2]

A commitment to excellence in product or service

This means day-by-day, month after month, year upon year striving to be and to give the best for the Master in quality and value. Excellence must be defined by the customer and shape their actual experiences with you.[3]

The leader will be involved in accountable relationships

As a business person ministers in the marketplace, Satan will be particularly active in trying to destroy the person and his ministry. It is a common axiom of the Christian life that the greater the ministry, the greater the attack. So building a godly defense against Satan becomes imperative for the Christian leader in the marketplace. Accountable relationships and group prayer with mature Christians are among the best defenses possible against the attacks of Satan.

In the book of Proverbs alone there are at least 24 direct references to the need and value of godly counsel. A lone sheep

---

1 See Appendix B on creating a "Strategic Plan for Ministry"
2 See Chapter 3: "Profits - New Light on an Old Topic"
3 See Chapter 10: "Excellence Is Your Only Choice"

is easy prey for even one wolf, let alone a pack. Our enemies travel in hordes and are determined to thwart any good work attempted, using guile and deceit. Our greatest defense is the multiplied eyes, ears, spirits and hearts of like-minded peers who are mature believers. The synergistic power of consistent open relationships focused on seeking godly power and direction can't be exaggerated and shouldn't be ignored.

A lone sheep will (not may) fall![4]

8 *An ongoing commitment to spiritual growth and development on the part of the Owner, President, CEO or whoever leads the firm*

Your company will never exceed your own spiritual level or depth of commitment. This means your personal spiritual growth is an essential prerequisite before anyone else will be influenced to grow through the efforts of your firm. The leader must practice daily Bible study, prayer and communion with God. This is generally best done the first thing each day.

Studying the lives of great Christians confirms this fact. I have never known, or heard of, a Christian used of God in truly meaningful ways for a long period of time who has not practiced a daily time of feeding on God's Word and communion with Him. They invariably say that such time and intimacy is the foundation and wellspring of their life in Christ. Effective ministry simply does not happen without personal spiritual growth!

For years I struggled with a commitment to spending the first part of each day with our Father, believing I could fit time in during the day or at night. Most days I did find such time and I believe I did grow. But at a certain point, God made clear to me that if He were truly first in my life He should deserve the first of my day. Somehow I knew that this guidance was serious and not to be taken lightly. I began to spend the first hour of each day with Him and now I understand what all the others who testified to the need and benefit of this time meant. It has changed my life forever in ways that not only I, but also others, can see.

I still spend the same time at night and find times during the day as before, but the real benefit and the truest time is based on this

---

4 See Appendix A on a "Personal Council of Advisors"

unwavering commitment early each morning. Before my mind can be assaulted by the world, with its diversions and urgencies, I meet with my Father, my older Brother, and my Counselor. I seek their guidance for my day and try to listen to them as they give it. My Father has given me a book He has written that I can use to know about the ways and plans that He and my older Brother have for our family business. My Counselor knows every word of this Book and He can explain any part I need. They all pull for me so hard and want me to succeed so badly. What a fool I would be not to show up for our times together.

There are certainly other practices of a company committed to serving Christ which we could discuss, but I believe they can be found rooted in these eight basics. For instance, wise Biblical stewardship and sound financial policies will come from understanding and applying God's Word, as will top-notch service and care for customers and employees. God's business plan is the best plan. He is no fool nor is His will ever foolish. What He asks us to do is always the best for all concerned. Crudely stated, "Obeying God is good business." These eight characteristics are simply practices that will encourage long-term knowledge and obedience to Him.

Each of our three legs of ministry will be progressively strengthened over time as we apply these basics. Many potentially great athletes fail because they do not apply the basic practices of training. So it is with us as we strive to operate our businesses to the glory of God. "And also if anyone competes in athletics, he is not crowned unless he competes according to the rules" (2 Timothy 2:5).

Chapter 7

How Do You Measure Success?

As business people we are trained to apply certain standards to track our progress or lack thereof according to the world's definition of success. These measurements carry terms like net profit, return on invested capital and market share. We know and understand that our success in the world's eyes is measured against our ability to make progress in these areas.

But we don't have any comparable metrics when it comes to measuring our success in operating a company for Christ and sharing God's love in the marketplace. This is an ironic situation since this is the one area of our business activity which will be eternally valuable.

It's hard for most of us to remember what our exact financial profits were and what we did with them last year, let alone five or ten years ago. That is because dollars really have a decreasing influence in our lives as time goes on. But the Lord promises that treasure laid up in heaven can never be lost. The truth is that how we handle the opportunities God puts before us will be important 100 or 1000 or a million years from now. That's a far cry from worldly profits which diminish each year in their ability to satisfy.

Given this reality, we should spend at least as much time planning, pursuing, and evaluating our success in achieving eternal profitability as we do earthly monetary profitability.

There are three basic metrics that any business can use to estimate its effectiveness in marketplace ministry. These are: our reputation within the body of Christ, our reputation with the unbelieving world, and our production of "eternal fruit." Over time, I believe that careful use and observation of these measurements will provide the kind of guidance we need just as surely as any profit and loss statement or balance sheet provides a financial barometer for a company.

Our Reputation Within the Body of Christ

The first indicator of our success in ministering through our company comes from our reputation within the body of Christ. If our reputation over time with our brothers and sisters in Christ is poor, we probably are failing in several areas. Our reputation is compromised if other Christians have bad things to say about their contacts with us. Such general opinions of our company might be expressed by thoughts such as, "They call themselves Christian, but their practices deny it."

This is not to say that we must always have good reports at all times. There are legitimate misunderstandings and even our best-intended actions can be misinterpreted by a few at any given point in time. But where there is smoke, there usually is a fire. When the testimony of other Christians is decidedly negative, it is probably justified in some sense.

The body of Christ, given time, will recognize and nurture that which is truly godly. It is, in fact, almost too prone to be forgiving and to overlook faults in a brother or sister.

It may be difficult to find out what people really think of your company. Most of your family, employees, friends and suppliers will have a hard time being honest with you. But you can learn what others really think of your business if you encourage open and accountable relationships, see the value in making the effort to find out the truth, and take the time to ask enough people several pointed questions. One thing is for sure; you need to know accurately how the body of Christ perceives you.

It is highly likely you are on the right track if your testimony to other believers is positive and an encouragement to them towards godliness in the marketplace.

Your reputation with believers is a very powerful leading and real-time indicator of your long-term success in marketplace ministry. Over time, if you are sincerely engaging in the eight practices of a Christian company given in the previous chapter, it will show clearly in your business and other Christians will recognize the positive results.

Our Reputation with the Unbelieving World

Obviously, unbelievers typically have a different basis for their opinions than do Christians. But their perceptions also have validity in measuring our success in marketplace ministry.

In giving the requirements for church leadership the Bible states that those qualified for such a position must have "a good testimony among those who are outside" (1Timothy 3:7). Mother Teresa was an example of someone who was universally respected for her actions, even by those who would totally reject her doctrine or even her Savior. What we do and how we do it speaks so loudly to unbelievers (and believers) that they can only truly hear our words when they echo our actions. They want to see our words lived out in our actions.

The world can spot greed, covetousness and manipulation of others as well or better than the church can. If they see that our primary motivation is the love of money, rather than concern for others, they will know it. It always shows.

If their impression of you and your business goes along the lines of, "They call themselves Christians but they are just like us, grubbing for a bigger piece of the pie to use for their own pleasures," they are probably right.

Again, this is not to say that they will always interpret our best actions and motives to be Christ-like. They definitely won't. Over time, however, if they don't see any difference in our companies, it's because there is no discernable difference. If Christ were literally running our firm, wouldn't the difference be unmistakable? Shouldn't we have the same goal?

You are probably on the right track if the typical non-Christian's view of your firm sounds something like this: "Well I don't understand them, they give away more than they keep, and they could earn a whole lot more if they weren't so darn soft and forgiving. But I've got to hand it to them; they are good people to do business with. They keep their word and they're not afraid to help where they can."

Remember, we're talking about impressions developed over an extended period of time. Our real values will always come out and be recognized over time.

Production of Eternal Fruit

This third measure of success in carrying Christ into the marketplace is highly dependent upon a good reputation both within and outside the Christian community.

"By this shall my Father is glorified, that you bear much fruit; so you will be my disciples," Jesus says in John 15:8.

Eternal fruit can be most simply and easily defined as "lives turned toward God."

The production of eternal fruit is accomplished by the way we do what we do and say what we say. It means that because of what we do and how we do it, in combination with what we say, others are influenced towards God. To oversimplify, our ministry involves being used by the Lord in delivering the "three S's": Salvation, Sanctification and Service.

When eternal fruit is being produced, some people will come to know Christ because of their contacts with our company. We will help introduce them to Christ. Because of something that happens between us, God uses us to make Himself known to them and they are saved. When salvation occurs, eternal fruit is being produced.

There is another kind of eternal fruit that is produced as we encourage others who already know Christ to know Him better and more intimately. This is discipleship or sanctification. There are dozens of ways we can teach, encourage, provide others an example, and inspire them. We produce eternal fruit as people come in contact with our business and us and therefore come into a closer relationship with Christ.

Unfortunately, some will not know God or even care to learn of Him despite their relationship with our firm. But they will experience the love and grace of God in our relationship with them. They may never acknowledge Him, but they will be helped or touched in a positive way because we serve them in His name. We may feed them, clothe them, or watch their kids while they work. We might visit them in jail or the hospital or provide medicine for them in the name of Jesus. In big or small ways they will receive blessings because we have first received blessing from Christ.

This is also a kind of eternal fruit. Don't discount its value. It is said that most people have heard the gospel as many as 10 times before they invite Christ into their lives. Which presentation is more important, the first or the last? Obviously they are equally vital.

Your actions can share the gospel just as surely as can another person's words. Maybe His love shown in your actions will be the first time someone actually learns of Jesus' love. Don't sell it short in the production of eternal fruit!

Eternal fruit that we know about or can observe is easy to measure. So this area of evaluating our success in marketplace ministry is a little easier to measure than such abstract things like reputation. People who get saved, come to Bible study or church, or enjoy meals we provide, can all be counted.

But there is yet another type of huge blessing that we know nothing about directly. As we set our hearts on serving God, many more are invariably touched than we will ever know. We can get a glimpse of this eternal fruit here on earth, but only in Heaven will we really know the true harvest.

Let me give you an example from our chemical business. We used to have a sign in front of our plant that displayed a simple, encouraging verse from the Bible. We changed it each week. The sign didn't seem to accomplish much and, due to various circumstances, we ultimately took it down. To our amazement, we immediately began to receive phone calls and letters from people who told us of what an encouragement it had been to them. Some even said that they drove miles out of their way to work to pass by and see what the verse would be each week. A single-parent police officer said she would come by at night and sometimes stop and pray by our building. "It helped to know that there were businessmen who cared for God," she said.

Producing eternal fruit through our business relationships is the true ministry focus of a company serving God in the marketplace. As ambassadors for Christ, we can and should plan for this fruit and work toward its production. Given its importance, it should be planned for and measured with at least as much zeal and concern as bottom-line profit, market share or any of the worldly measurements of our business.

The C12 Group, LLC has a wonderful tool called *A Strategic Plan for Ministry* that can be a real help in getting started (see Appendix B). This workbook is designed to incorporate the principles used in making a business plan to create a plan for producing eternal fruit through the business.

Here are some questions each Christian running a company needs to ask before it is too late. You need to ask these questions now, because someday the answers will be all that is left of your business that has any eternal value to you:

- Have you thought about measuring fruitfulness in your business relationships?
- How many people have been saved in the last year because they met and dealt with you or one of your people in business?
- How many other Christians have you helped or encouraged to grow?
- Has any hungry or hurting person been fed or cared for because you run a company for God?

Read the 15th chapter of the book of John. Think about what it means to be a branch attached to a vine, designed to bear fruit. Think about how being attached to the vine relates to bearing fruit in and through our companies. Think about what He promises will happen to branches that don't bear fruit.

Your success as a company designed to bear fruit in the marketplace is being measured every day. It would be good to have an accurate idea of where you stand!

WORKING YOUR MINISTRY

It might be easier if we took a very legalistic approach to running a company for Jesus Christ. Then we could just say, "the Bible says to do this and don't do that." But it wouldn't necessarily always be true. That's just not the way things work when complications and our imperfect judgment are involved. Only He can judge or inspire you perfectly!

There isn't just *one* way to run a company for Christ, but there *are* some general Biblical principles that, if applied in the unique circumstances of your business, will help to develop His way forward for you. The following section is designed to outline some Scripturally-consistent principles addressing the three major components of our testimony: how we handle people, how we handle money, and how we handle the quality of our products or services. We cannot be exhaustive here, but we can provide some practical, observable, "doable" guidelines to get you started in running your company for Christ.

You may not be able to do very much at first. If so, do not be discouraged. After all, if you have spent years pretending that you are in charge of your company, it will take time to change to the new "operating system" where you are merely an "employee" of The King. Just beginning to take action on any of these points will result in the Lord showing you other areas where you can join in with Him and follow His lead. Remember, "the journey of a thousand miles begins with but a single step!"

As you begin this journey, recall that what we really are talking about relates not just to WHAT you do but more so to the COMMITMENT of running your company for Christ. If the commitment is there, you will respond to the Lord's leading in what you do. Commitment comes first (2 Corinthians 8:5)!

Assuming that the commitment is already there, let's turn specifically toward what to do. Since God is more interested in people than money or things, let's start with some principles of personnel management.

Chapter 8

PEOPLE ARE FOREVER

Most business people, whether Christian or not, do not put nearly enough effort into selecting employees and then dealing wisely with them. This applies across the entire spectrum, from very highly paid executives to minimum wage hourly workers and everyone in between.

People are your most important and valuable asset. As the leader you are responsible to God for their care. You can never pour too much time, effort, or money into their development. I have never heard a CEO say he just wished his people were less enthused, happy, involved, well-trained, knowledgeable, qualified, or productive! How about it? Have you?

The needs of your employees should be prayed over regularly (1 John 5:14-15). A successful employee is indeed a good and perfect gift (James 1:17). This facet of building a successful company is vastly undervalued. Nothing short of God's miraculous favor is of more value to a company than having the right person in the right place at the right time and, especially, having the right heart.

Conversely, few things offer a greater burden or hindrance in building a strong company than poor hiring and placement. The devil often uses our lack of attention and diligence in this area to infiltrate our ranks with divisive and unprofitable people. They can drain the joy and strength from others and can really ruin an otherwise good company and its witness.

The Christian testimony of too many companies and managers is damaged because not enough care and prayer are put into managing, developing, and communicating with employees. The situation is just about as bad in most companies owned by Christians as in the typical secular company.

We need to pray consistently that God will bring us His perfect candidates, even when no jobs are currently available. In our business we grew from seven to 55 employees in six years without ever running an ad or using a placement service. Talented specialists, such as highly skilled analytical chemists, plant laborers, sales people, and a comptroller, appeared as a result of diligent prayer.

We initiated and maintained a file of resumes of those who applied, often long before we even knew we needed them. Not everyone was acceptable, but an unusually high percentage were hired from this unsolicited pool of applicants. When the business was sold after 10 years, there was still a surplus of qualified people applying to work with our company.

Employees

The basic obligations that management has to all employees are:

- Proper selection and placement done in harmony with the needs of the job and the gifts and talents of the person.

- Explaining to them exactly what they are expected to do.

- Being certain they are trained and equipped to do it.

- Letting them know how they are performing in management's eyes.

So many problems, especially in small growth companies, result from communication failures. Often people think they are doing well, but their boss thinks otherwise. In many instances the boss is delighted with an employee, but refuses to hare the necessary praise and compliments. Either situation can lead to damaged relationships, poor productivity and added cost for the business.

In many such companies the customers get constant, caring attention, equipment is spotless, and the grounds are maintained perfectly. The leaders of these same companies seem to care more about customers and machines than about their own people. This is not Biblical or practical.

Handling your employees well is a key area for "shoe leather Christianity." It takes persistent effort and is not nearly as glamorous as product development or sales. Often this can be a complex area, full of frustration and without fully satisfactory answers. That is why so many Christian business leaders ignore individual and team development issues until there is an obvious problem. Usually the problem becomes obvious too late and unnecessary damage has already been done to the organization and to the Christian testimony of its leaders.

If Jesus Christ were to come back in the flesh to operate a business, the first area he would focus on in many companies would be improved personnel management. Let me personalize that thought and suggest that you ask yourself honestly, "Are personnel issues the first thing Christ would address in my business?" If so, you need to immediately begin praying about your personnel situation and how it can be improved. After all, if Christ owns your business, then the Owner sets the priorities for His company. Our job as stewards is to carry out the Owner's wishes.

Building a winning team is often a complex, difficult, frustrating and slow process for many business owners. But there is one unchanging guideline we can suggest. Every time you need to make any decision, before you make it, ALWAYS ask yourself: "What would Jesus do in this situation?"

It is amazing how often you will be able to crystallize a very clear idea of what He would do in your situation. It also amazing how often you will not like the answer. Our preference for "pragmatism" in the moment is often not His way. Making decisions His way can seem hard, but this always works best in the long run.

Personnel Management Principles

Here are some general personnel management principles that should be part of every company run for Christ:

1. The company needs to have a Statement of Purpose and communicate that purpose clearly and consistently to its employees. The Christian company needs to follow its purpose statement in all it says and does.

   As Tom Peters states in *A Passion for Excellence*, "To your employees you *are* your acted-out priorities."

   In the long run, your employees will be happier, more fulfilled and more committed to a successful career with your company if they have something bigger than a paycheck to work for and identify with. A proper Statement of Purpose can serve as a rallying point, true motivation, inspiration, a helpful arbiter and a corrector of behavior. It must capture and articulate your vision, your "grand purpose." People long to know the significance of their work, to feel that they are contributing to something bigger than the daily effort it takes!

Proverbs 29:18 reminds us, that "Where there is no vision, the people perish."[1] One of our primary jobs as leaders is to **clearly articulate vision and purpose**.

2. Every team member needs to have a **clear job description** and must know and understand what is expected of them (Proverbs 22:3). Many business leaders fear job descriptions because they believe they can be self-limiting and have a potentially negative impact if used to avoid doing what needs to be done. This concern merely warrants writing job descriptions as a set of clear guidelines with mutually beneficial flexibility built-in. Ending the description with "and other tasks and duties which are assigned from time to time" often can cover such contingencies.

3. Every employee should have **regular performance reviews**. These reviews are used to make sure the manager and the employee understand each other as it relates to assigned work and how the employee is doing. Performance reviews also provide the perfect opportunity to keep in contact with the employee's personal needs. The performance review should be seen as a wonderful opportunity for ministry and communication. It is the time when all kinds of topics can be raised in a caring and encouraging atmosphere. As Christians, we are commanded to "speak the truth in love" (Ephesians 4:15). Some companies may also allow employees to review their managers, perhaps as a part of a "360 degree" review process. Good performance must be measurable to be meaningful.

4. **Hire based on character and capabilities**. People should be selected on the basis of their gifts, training and qualifications, not just because they are Christians, friends or fellow church members who need a job. Any deviations from this guideline should be carefully monitored. If a person is to be placed in a job as a method of giving aid or helping them, the immediate supervisor and all other employees need to be in agreement. Don't try to delegate your ministry burden. It will not work. Include those impacted in the decision. "Like an archer who wounds everyone, so is he who hires a fool or hires those who pass by," warns Proverbs 26:10 (NAS). Seek positive character

---

1 Guidelines for creating a viable purpose statement are included in *A Strategic Plan for Ministry* and can be obtained from The C12 Group, LLC.

qualities as diligently as technical competence. Many fall short here. Many more people fail because of character failure than fail due to incompetence.

5. An **employee handbook**, properly done, is an immense help. Important factors are written and clear. It can save much time and trouble in communicating the essentials, and is an important way to emphasize the primary values, purposes and policies of the company to its employees.

6. **Communication** at all levels is vital. Relationships among persons at all levels are valued and guarded by good, clear, consistent and frequent communications. Self-serving politics are not tolerated and it is extremely important that the leader lead by example in this area (Philippians 2:3-4).

7. Competition is encouraged only against the standard of an individual becoming the best he or she can be. Personal development and improvement are the criteria, not pitting one employee against another. **Teamwork** is truly valued and all employees are invited to offer suggestions. The leader has to be willing to demonstrate by his or her actions that such suggestions really are valued (Romans 14:12,19).

8. **Authority and responsibility** are given equally, with neither out of balance. Few things are more frustrating for anyone than being held responsible for something without having the authority to correctly deal with it. God never holds us responsible for what He doesn't give us authority over (Isaiah 61:8a).

9. Personnel **problems are resolved Biblically** and there is emphasis on using the company to help with personal problems (Matthew 18:15-17, Proverbs 18:24, Colossians 3:12-14, 2 Corinthians 5:18-20). As Christians, we have been given the ministry of reconciliation as ambassadors for Christ. Reconciling workplace differences is a great place to apply Biblical principles, provide shepherding/discipling, and display both grace and truth.

10. **Training** is plentiful, consistent, valued and utilized in the development of both spiritual and functional capabilities. The deep eternal values of the company are stressed. Eternal fruit is valued above profit, and accomplishment in both areas is

recognized and pursued. Proverbs 22:6 exhorts us to "train up a child in the way he should go." We are not parents to our employees, but the principle applies just the same. There are very similar patterns in good parenting and good personnel management.

11. **Discipline**, when needed, is carried out promptly according to predetermined processes (Ecclesiastes 8:11). Clearly written communication concerning potential causes of discipline is essential. Establish clear ground rules and use them consistently (Proverbs 13:14).

12. **Compensation** should be fair (i.e., competitive or slightly above) but not excessive (James 5:4, Jeremiah 22:13). By personally setting the example, the CEO testifies to his real values and beliefs in this area.

13. Whenever possible **promotion** should be from within (Proverbs 13:12). This policy yields widespread secondary benefits (e.g., positive culture, loyalty, continuous learning) in a growing firm.

14. Proper and consistent adherence to many of the guidelines outlined above will minimize firing or releasing. When such action is necessary, it will be the obvious result of being unable to find a reasonable remedial alternative. Firing or releasing an employee is a normal result of either following the performance evaluation process or a violation of clear company rules.

    When **termination** is the result of unsatisfactory performance, the employee should be out-placed by management using whatever helpful tools may be available. Concern should be expressed *and demonstrated* for the employee even while acknowledging that they may no longer have a role at your firm. It is your job as the leader to model healthy concern for all people - even employees who are dismissed.

Your most immediate workplace ministry in sharing the love of Christ is with your employees. Each leader in a Christian company is responsible before God for the people under their care and direction. How we interact with them has tremendous influence on their lives. Personnel management may not be glamorous, but it is critically important in building a company that exhibits a strong witness for Christ.

Beyond our employees, our dealings and relationships with customers, suppliers and trade associates demonstrates the character and priorities of our business. How we actually deal with them will tell them more about the true place of Christ in our lives than anything we can say. Abraham Lincoln has been quoted as saying, "Sir, what you are speaks so loudly I cannot hear a word you are saying." 150 years later, I still get the message loud and clear.

Suppliers

For many of us, the employees of our suppliers represent a large portion of our extended value-chain and "workforce." Here are some further "people principles" to consider when dealing with your suppliers:

1. Suppliers are treated according to the Golden Rule and not abused or taken advantage of unfairly. Long-term mutually beneficial relationships are valued and promoted. The positive contributions of suppliers are recognized at least as quickly as their failings. Good suppliers are a gift from God, just like good employees. We need to pray for them, cultivate their support, support them and at times forgive them.

2. Unless we welcome being treated in the same way, we should not unfairly play one supplier against another to their detriment. This is a radical prescription, but remember, we are all suppliers to someone. To use tactics on our suppliers that we would complain about when used on us by our customers is pure hypocrisy. There are many other mutually agreeable ways to establish competitive cost targets and continuous improvement (e.g., fair bidding, competitive benchmarking, value engineering, long-term performance contracts, etc.)

3. Suppliers should be given as much information about our requirements as they need to do their jobs to our satisfaction. It is unfair to give them less. Clearly stated expectations (e.g., quality, delivery, cost) and operating targets are essential if we are to be on the same team and build a healthy long-term supply relationship.

4. Disclosing one supplier's price to force down another's price should be avoided. Suppliers should be encouraged to give their best effort and price the first time and further price negotiations

should generally be discouraged. It is not always possible to completely avoid these things, but minimizing them will aid in building healthy, stable, long-term relationships. Getting the lowest price doesn't always mean making the best deal. Using unkind or inconsiderate tactics to gain "rock-bottom" pricing is short-term thinking and usually not Christ-like.

5. We must treat the representatives of our suppliers and potential suppliers with at least as much courtesy and respect as we would hope our representatives would receive when they interact with our customers. Otherwise we are gross hypocrites. We cannot treat our supplier's sales people poorly and then complain when someone else does the same to our sales representatives. Keeping appointments, being on time, providing respectful treatment at all times, and communicating the necessary details of our requirements are simply minimums. Supplier appreciation award banquets, periodic written recognition and encouragement, and occasional personal interface (e.g., dinner or office visit) are just the initial steps in going the second mile.

Customers

Turning to customers for a moment, remember that they too are people who deserve your respect. You would not think we would have to say that. But the truth is that most companies see their customers not as people, but as objects to be manipulated for profit or personal gain. They are seen as obstacles to be overcome, rather than people to be served. When they are manipulated, rather than ministered to, relationships built on these perceptions tend to become adversarial in nature. Adversarial relationships normally are not productive in sharing the love of God. Here are some further thoughts on dealing with customers:

1. Never do to any customer what you would object to having a supplier do to you (Matthew 7:12).

2. Never intentionally encourage a customer to do anything to his own hurt or detriment. We are to avoid being "stumbling blocks," even inadvertent ones, to those we touch (see 1 Corinthians 8:9). Christian, this means that using or encouraging excessive drinking (or perhaps any alcohol at all), promiscuous sex in any form, or bribing to solicit or secure business is ungodly

and unacceptable. Do not be deceived. God can never bless sin; it will always work against you and anyone involved in it. Rather, let your light shine as you build long-term, mutually beneficial relationships with your customers based on quality of service, value, product integrity, honesty, and acts done in love. Does that sound preachy? Well, take it up with the Boss!

3. Since you cannot truly win an argument with a customer (no one ever has), cultivate listening to them instead. Proactively engage them by listening and ask God to show you creative and unique ways to meet customers' needs. Stop *selling* them and start listening and *serving* them. Focus groups, inter-company visits, staff exchange visits and mutual celebrations all encourage the kinds of relationships that lead to mutual understanding and exchange.

4. Aim to develop trust. It takes time and cumulative shared experiences for trust to ripen. After all, if you never have had the opportunity to violate trust, no one really knows if you can be trusted or not.

5. See your customers as the valuable asset that they are. Remember, your income statement and paycheck are fueled by their dollars. As we all know, it is far less costly to retain existing satisfied customers than to constantly recruit replacements!

Also remember that every customer's soul is as important to Jesus as yours or any native's in the most remote jungle on earth. Jesus died for your customers as well, and He loves them. They are as precious to Him as you are. Treat them as He would.

Competitors

Even our competitors and trade associates contribute to our overall testimony. A few thoughts on competitors:

1. Never gossip about competitors or say anything derogatory. Rather, find ways to give good reports (Proverbs 25:21-22; Matthew 5:44-45).

2. Pray *for*, not *about*, your competitors.

3. Treat them as you believe Jesus would treat them. Apply the rule of reacting in the opposite spirit to them. Whatever negative you see in them, show them the opposite "positive" attitude.

4. Above all, be the kind of competitor that you would like them to be. Be an example to them.

People, people, people! Everything we do involves them somehow. All that we do affects others either in a positive or negative way. It's a little like the person watching a golf match who said, "Every shot makes someone happy."

Increasing our awareness of how we treat people will strengthen our business and our testimony. The greatest companies and ministries are hyper people-oriented, user-friendly organizations. People or organizations that are not so people-oriented can easily become losers. Time spent working on improving our relationships with others is never wasted and has a huge potential payback, both now and in eternity.

Chapter 9

FINANCES SHOW THE REAL "YOU"

Violating God's principles for financial management is the single largest reason companies owned by Christians fail. They fail at the "bottom line" both financially and spiritually. They fail financially in many cases because of excessive borrowing and debt. And they often fail at the spiritual bottom line as bad financial strategies wipe out much of the good Christian testimony they have built up in other areas.

The money arena is typically where people are quick to notice our actions versus our words. Finances are a challenging area for almost everyone, Christians included. It is especially hard for those with the authority to establish or control financial arrangements. If the love of money is present, it will become apparent in our approach to financial management.

For decades it has been an assumed business best practice to build a company through leverage, borrowing someone else's money to maximize potential return on shareholders equity. This boils down to gambling that the profits earned will enable the company to pay its usual operating expenses and also repay the loan with interest. This approach works sometimes. Unfortunately, it doesn't work all the time. In our increasing leveraged society, it seems like it is working less and less. And when this strategy fails, it typically fails suddenly and spectacularly, with scores of people wounded.

Even when leverage works, the testimony of the growth of the business does not always relate to God's supply but to the banks'. Borrowing, especially as the world practices it, is designed to turn our dependence away from God's provision and causes us to look to the world's system for our supply. A stewards and His undershepherds, we must be aware of our true motivations and the potential consequences of such decisions.

There are other options versus borrowing to build business. We have all but lost the concept of building a business through reinvestment of its profits. When outside capital is needed, you might also consider "sharing" part of your business through the sale of stock or a portion of your firm to a "qualified" buyer.[1]

Jesus *warned* in the parable of the sower (see Matthew 13) against the "deceitfulness of riches."

The potential for deception is in most of us and we need to have the objective perspective of others to help control and defeat it in our lives. That's one reason why peer accountability groups and councils of advisors, such as the C12 Group, are so important. They help protect us from our own weaknesses.

Let's get one thing straight: God is not "into" money. He uses it, but He is not in any way measured by it. Money is not a necessary part of His Kingdom. It is used only on earth, not in heaven.

God has not chosen to demonstrate His power and love by making companies owned and run by Christians large and successful. If He had, the largest and most successful companies in the world would all be owned and run by Christians. Obviously this is not even close to being the case. As we all know, the wealthiest people, businesses, and nations of this world are not particularly Christian.

If God's testimony depended on the wealth of His followers, Christians would be the wealthiest people in the world. If you really want to influence people for God, let the character of Christ be formed in you. This happens as you pursue righteousness, godliness, faith, love, patience, gentleness, and seek first the Kingdom of God.

You can do this through your business and let money take care of itself. Use money wisely, from God's perspective, but don't let it use you. This doesn't mean that financial profits, banking relationships, or effective use of capital markets are unimportant. It just means that the testimony to God from our business is *more* important than profits per se.

Our purpose here is not to provide an exhaustive guide to Christian business finance. The desire is to make us all aware of financial pitfalls and how important our financial strategy is to our success in promoting the Kingdom of God through our businesses. Here are some general principles concerning finances from God's perspective:

---

1 See Chapter 9: Number 4 on partnerships (page 53).

1. The Bible does not prohibit debt but it does contain several warnings concerning debt and borrowing. Therefore debt is to be avoided or used only at God's direct permission or direction. Excess debt is not permitted. What is excess debt? Perhaps anything over one month's receivables or any amount beyond what you know you can repay (Habakkuk 2:6-7, Proverbs 22:7, Romans 13:8). There are at least three important Biblical principles that bear on the inherent dangers in borrowing:

   a. Presuming upon the future (James 4:13-14). Committing to future repayment implicitly assumes that cash flow will be available to meet the agreed obligations. Yet no man knows what the future will bring. We must plan with diligence and a keen awareness of our limitations.

   b. God, as owner of your business, holds you accountable for the assets entrusted to you as steward. Subjecting those assets unwisely to loss is poor stewardship.

   c. Being enslaved to debt places you, the borrower, in bondage. "The borrower is servant to the lender," warns Proverbs 22:7. "No one can serve two masters. Either he will hate the one and love the other, or he will be devoted to one and despise the other," Jesus warned in the Sermon on the Mount. One cannot be devoted to both God and lenders.

2. Personal guarantees should be avoided. If you have already personally guaranteed loans, then make plans to either pay the loans off or eliminate the personal guarantees. Loans that are completely collateralized without personal guarantee are the only acceptable loans. The Bible is very clear in this area. It describes personally guaranteeing a loan as pledging "surety." So many small business owners have been trapped here (Proverbs 6:1-5, 11:15, 22:26-27 and 27:13).

3. Creditors of the business are given equal claims on money generated as are the employees and both come *before* the owner or CEO (Psalm 37:21, Proverbs 3:27-28).

4. Formal financial partnerships and shared ownership *with non-believers* are to be avoided (2 Corinthians 6:14-15). It is important to note that the Bible does not say that we should

not do business with or have agreements with non-believers. But the Bible says we shouldn't be "yoked" to them. What is a yoke? A yoke is something from which you can't walk away. You are tied to it giving up your freedom to act independently. One can't be totally free to obey God if he is yoked to another who holds a different perspective on reality.

Obviously this does not preclude a Christian owning stock in a non-Christian business or investing in things of all acceptable types as long as he has not borrowed to make this investment or otherwise "yoked" himself to it. If God asks him to, he can drop it and walk away.

5. Sales agreements, licenses, and contracts are also possible yokes. We need to be very careful in any alliance we make. Our name can be damaged by the actions of others. We can't always control or avoid these things, so proceed with caution.

6. Pricing is done honestly and in such a way to avoid being guilty of using unjust weights and measures (Proverbs 20:23). This occurs when we mask our actual pricing or unfairly sell the same products or services, in the same quantity and quality, to different people for different prices. This can cheat those who pay the higher price and damage the reputation of the one dealing in this way (Proverbs 11:1 and 16:11). Transparency and fairness are called for.

7. A written policy covering the granting of credit and making collections should be in place and followed consistently. Credit extension is an area where many companies are slack and hurt themselves greatly. They miss many opportunities to explicitly show and share the love of Christ and exercise poor stewardship of God's money as well. Many times a simple misunderstanding or service problem can be cleared up, removing the root cause of the payment delay, with sincere interpersonal contact.

8. When a company cannot pay a bill or meet a commitment, a responsible person should contact the creditor immediately. The person should give an honest explanation of the problem and explain how/when they will be paid. A company owned by a Christian does not wait for the creditor to call, but accepts the responsibility to initiate the contact and keep their end of

the relationship clear and honest.

We always want to show the difference that being a company for Christ makes. A company that takes the initiative in keeping its end of all agreements to pay will be noticed "big time" in our marketplace where defaults are becoming so common (Proverbs 28:13).

9. Profits are shared with those helping to create them and with other Christian ministries. A generous and giving heart will also be noticed, as will a greedy and self-serving one (Proverbs 11:24-25, Luke 6:38).

10. Wages are fair but not excessive. It is not necessary to be the highest paying company to have a good testimony nor is it good to be the lowest. Extremes, as in most other things, are best avoided. We want to create cultures based on performance, not entitlement. Money is just one of many reasons employees choose an employer! Contemporary studies reveal that pay rates rank near the middle of the "top ten" reasons why employees select a particular employer.

11. If the company enters into a contract, it will keep it even if it hurts (Psalm 15:4b)! This does not mean that a Christian company cannot or will not ask to be released from an unfair or undesirable agreement. But if it is unable to obtain permission from the other party to alter or eliminate the agreement, then they will keep it without complaint.

A Christian company's word must be good. It will keep its word even if it hurts. How can we testify that God's Word can be trusted if our own word is unreliable?

12. The owner's compensation is set fairly in proportion to the compensation of the team and may be set by his council of advisors, accountability group or board's compensation committee. This is an area where the attitude and personal example of the leader is tremendously powerful. Their motives and values will be seen via their approach to personal compensation perhaps more quickly and clearly by others in the company than in any other area. Our world today is perversely money motivated and controlled. So when someone comes along exhibiting God's eternal values rather than the world's, they really stand out from the crowd. And that's what

the Christian business owner or CEO should do - stand out like a "light set upon a hill."

I learned years ago in a Bill Gothard seminar that my children would likely do in excess what I allowed myself in moderation. Our employees are not children, but I think that the principle nevertheless applies. Those who look to us for leadership will tend to copy and exaggerate our traits. This seems two or three times as true when applied to negative or harmful things. Materialism and the love of money is devastating our society, our country and even the church in America. There is a desperate need for leaders and companies who can demonstrate a godly attitude toward financial management.

The Christian business CEO, Owner or President is in a unique position to effectively stand against our culture's "more is better, most is best" temporal mentality. God's leaders in God's companies have tremendous opportunities for influence through their approach to financial management.

Chapter 10

EXCELLENCE—
THE ONLY CHOICE

> *"Do you see a man who excels in his work?*
> *He will stand before kings;*
> *He will not stand before unknown men."*
>   *Proverbs 22:29 (NIV)*

Running a company for Christ requires a sincerely demonstrated commitment to excellence in all that your company does. There simply is no alternative. Excellence is like honesty: it is a necessary part of the foundation of your company if it is to serve Christ.

We cannot even begin to calculate the enormous value, both now and in eternity, of pursuing excellence for Christians running a business as a platform for ministry. Likewise, we devastate our Christian testimony in immeasurable ways via poor quality, service or workmanship and an indifferent attitude.

Those who do excellent work have always been respected by every society. A committed craftsman is inevitably admired and, in our own lives, we seek to do business with those we recognize as being excellent or exceptionally good at what they do. We strongly tend to give respect to those who provide us with excellence. We listen to their opinions and recommend them to others. But who listens to someone whose products or services are shoddy? We don't give them much credibility or referral business, do we?

But what is "excellence"? Is excellence only found in high-priced goods and services where price is not an object? Can someone whose business deals with "low end" or commodity products and entry-level customers also be "excellent"?

It is very important for us to have a healthy understanding of excellence from a Christian perspective. I propose the following for a working definition of excellence for a Christian:

"Excellence is being the very best that God created you to be and never willingly settling for less."

This may not mean that you are truly the best in the world at whatever you do. But it does mean that you will be the best YOU can be. Excellence is achieving your maximum God-given potential, progressively moving toward the highest utilization of all you have been sovereignly entrusted with. For instance, the tender young bud of a flower is as excellent as a flower in full bloom. They don't look the same or provide the same function, but they are both equally excellent in God's eyes.

For Christians the ultimate definition of excellence is in God's eyes. If we are obediently becoming all He created us to be, we are excellent. The good news is that in God's kingdom all can be excellent. It is not necessarily easy to be excellent in God's eyes, but it is possible for everybody. While we who are saved are already viewed as spotless through the completed work of Christ on our behalf, we still have a lifetime of opportunities to grow in our performance as His ambassadors, stewards, and servant leaders.

For us, excellence begins when we commit what we do to the Lord and do it for Him, believing that He cares and will reward us as we do so (Colossians 3:22, Ephesians 6:6-8). We accept His standards and His ways, and as we do, we will naturally be drawn to excellence because no one is more excellent than our God, the very definition of perfection.

Over the years much business literature has been written concerning excellence. In my opinion, the best has been *A Passion for Excellence* by Tom Peters and Nancy Austin. Their analysis of why the best companies are so much superior to their competitors is well worth reading. There is a pleasant surprise for Christians in the book, as the best companies profiled by Peters display many of the qualities that the Bible extols, urges and commands us to follow.

There is nothing new under the sun. Often the "modern" world thinks it has discovered some new truth only to find that it really is only God's timeless truth freshly applied to the world's contemporary context. Excellence is, in its essence, God's truth applied to the world.

Here are some basic practices and commitments that lead to excellence in any company:

1. **A commitment to excellence is articulated and demonstrated.** Excellence is not just talk, but is lived out. People who contribute to it are recognized and rewarded. Unwavering commitment to excellence is a part of every decision concerning products, service, methods and people.

2. The company **stands squarely behind its products and services** and, where possible, offers a money-back or satisfaction guarantee. It may not always be possible to offer such a guarantee but few things speak louder to customers than your willingness to give up your profit until they are satisfied. There are many ways to work this out, and they all give a positive message concerning your integrity and commitment to your customer. Yes, occasionally someone takes advantage of you, but in the long run many more quality people will be attracted and repeat buyers encouraged.

3. **Complaints are recognized as possible opportunities for witnessing and handled as a priority.** Our way of handling dissatisfied customers or problems is a great chance to show them the difference Jesus Christ makes in a life.

   Most customers are lost over simple problems that are handled with indifference. They are not lost over tough problems that are hard to solve! In reality, every complaint is an opportunity to once again show our customers why they should choose to do business with us. This will be a very large contributor to your company's image in the marketplace. You will also benefit from a reduction in "silent defectors" from your customer base.

   Companies that try to avoid or ignore customer complaints are not excellent companies. Don't be defensive. Everyone makes mistakes. Excellent companies truly capitalize on theirs.

4. **Accountability for quality and excellence is established and maintained.** Accountability makes things happen. You can expect what you are willing to inspect. Someone has to be accountable and responsible for the excellence of your company and God has decided that it is you. You can delegate, but at the end of the day it will still be your responsibility. Don't let others delegate up. Establish and maintain accountability.

5. The company recognizes that **excellence is defined by the customer** and does not try to force its own convenient definition on them (Philippians 2:3-4). Many fail to listen when their customers tell them in various ways what would truly represent excellence in thier market niche. The market, not our internal rationalizations, determines excellence. Soliciting information from and listening to the customer is a trait shared by excellent companies. The leader must be personally committed to continually understanding what excellence really is as it changes over time. You must demonstrate your concern and sponsor on-going processes to remain "current."

6. **Innovation is constantly sought and rewarded.** A powerful enemy of excellence is "we've always done it this way." Always seeking a better way to serve more people keeps us sharp and open to genuine improvement. We serve a creative God. Unleash Him and let Him show you how fruitful you can be.

Encourage your team (even if you are the only one on it) to spend time looking for innovation. Don't just trust that it will happen. Plan for it. Set time apart to seek it. Constantly challenge the fundamentals and your underlying assumptions about the business. No matter how good or how bad things are, they can be comparatively better with sustained, purposeful innovation. Without innovation you are doomed to a slow death. Companies that don't innovate are sooner or later overtaken and pushed out of the market by those who do.

7. **Customers are served**, not merely manipulated for profit. Excellent companies do not see customers as inconveniences or obstacles to be overcome, but as potential recipients of ministry. For most of us this requires a very big change in our mind-set and, very likely, our budgeting, training and methods. Until we see our customers as people to be served, we will never become excellent or highly effective in sharing the love of God with them. Our customers typically make up the largest segment of our ministry mission field.

Every customer that God sends to us is someone we can touch for His Kingdom. But we probably won't get the chance, much less recognize it, if we are only looking at them as a source of cash flow. Customers are, of course, the method God uses to bring revenue to our business. But for a Christian company, customers should be viewed as opportunities for ministry first and sources of profits second. Excellent companies value their customers and serve them, they don't manipulate them.

8. Excellence requires that you **understand your product and business model and their relative standing in the marketplace**. What passes as excellent today may not be excellent tomorrow. Excellence means making the effort to remain truly informed and ahead of the served market changes that always come. Be sure to continually "benchmark" whatever is currently perceived as "best practice" in your served industry. Your customers want and deserve the latest and best products, technologies and services available.

The goal of an excellent company is to provide more for less than any competitor and have the customer recognize it. "Value plus" is always our goal. Obviously, it is not always possible for this to be the case, but it *can* always be the case, whatever the circumstances. When such excellence is the shared goal of your teams, good things happen (Philippians 3:13-14). A corporate culture that encourages a work attitude and ethic "as unto the Lord" is the sort of atmosphere that serves its customers and has enormous impetus toward excellence. We are called to excellence by our most excellent Creator. He looked at all that He had made and was able to say, "It is good." Let it be the desire of our hearts to do our work with His same Spirit and offer it to Him as an excellent offering.

A Light Shines Bright in Babylon

A PARABLE OF TWO MEN

We each have a platform. As we live, we build on it...day-by-day, moment-by-moment. The platform is established when we receive Jesus Christ as Lord and Savior and are born anew into His Kingdom. We build on it with our life, our works, the things we do. Some of the things we do have value in this life only, some have value here and also in eternal life in heaven, and some in heaven only.

We build on the platform of our salvation either eternal rewards or eternal loss. We build on it in our homes, our communities, our relationships and in our business lives.

As this applies to our business lives, hear now a parable of two men...

The first man was a janitor. He worked for the same company all of his working life, more than 40 years. He never rose above the position of janitor and never had anyone report to him. He never owned a home, never had an investment or bought a new car. In fact, he seldom traveled away from the city where he had lived all his life.

He was a fine janitor. All of the areas for which he was responsible were maintained according to the highest standards. The brass shone, the windows glistened, and the carpets were never dirty. He would occasionally be seen on his hands and knees, with a toothbrush, cleaning the corners the mop couldn't reach, where the floor and the tile wall met.

He always had a smile and a cheerful good word for the employees. After he retired, several folks remarked that they had never once heard him complain.

Over the 40 years, from time to time, he would be asked, "How come you work so hard? You don't really have to put in all that extra effort."

He would answer, "You don't understand. I'm doing this work for

Jesus and for Him it has got to be good. You see, He is my best friend. I love Him and owe Him my best because He gave His life for me."

Some of these people laughed and some just passed by. But some said, "Jesus? Your friend? I don't know about that. How can Jesus be a friend? I don't know Him in that way."

The janitor would always smile when this happened, and no one ever missed the love in his eyes when he answered, "Well, let me tell you about me and Jesus." He was never too busy to tell them how the love of his Lord had touched his life.

The second man worked for the same company. In fact, he had also worked there for more than 40 years. He and the janitor started at about the same time. The second man started right out of college. He had attended a fine university and had done well. He made good grades, worked hard and his parents were proud of him and how he had used the opportunity they had provided.

He joined the company in the sales department and quickly became the leading salesman in his department. In record time he was promoted, becoming the youngest sales manager, regional manager, vice president of sales and finally the youngest ever CEO of the corporation.

Under his leadership, the company grew and expanded, eventually becoming an international leader in its industry. The firm acquired other companies and, under his shrewd and wise direction, these companies prospered as well.

He was active in many civic organizations and government advisory panels. He was elected to the board of regents of his university and was a respected member of a fine church. He and his family could almost always be seen Sunday morning seated in the fourth row on the left side for the 11 a.m. service.

Unfortunately, even though he might have wished otherwise, his other activities kept him too busy to attend Wednesday night services or to participate in any of the ministries of the church. And travel often kept him away from home altogether.

Because of his obvious skills, gifts, and success, he was often asked to speak to organizations and groups. Other peer CEO's would even visit and inquire about how he had done so well.

He always gave the same answer, "This is the greatest land in the world and the opportunities are limitless. America is the land of freedom to excel and I've worked very hard. What I have done, you can too, if you believe you can and give your all."

Sometime when he was young, his father had told him, "Son, two things you cannot mix with your business: politics and religion. They are like oil and water and they just don't mix." It never occurred to him to question his father's advice, although deep in his heart he knew it just didn't seem right.

He was so busy there was not much time to think. With the business, the cottage at the beach, the club memberships for golf and tennis (when he could find time) and trying to fit family ski trips in between board meetings, his time flew by. Admired by multitudes, he retired after a long and successful career.

It happened that both men died on the same day. Just as the Scripture promises to each believer (1 Corinthians 3:11), each of the two men went to stand before Jesus to give an account of what they had done in the Body.

The CEO went first, as usual, and stepped before the Lord. Jesus put His hand on his shoulder and said to him, "My son, you have done well with your life. I gave you intelligence and opportunity. You worked hard and you took advantage of all that I set before you. You accomplished much, but son, all that you built must remain behind. Your homes and cars, your company and clubs were good, but they are not a part of my Kingdom. The university that you loved and served, refused to honor me and it will burn up and be destroyed. Your money is not needed here. My son, you labored long and hard, but foolishly. You have gained the good, but missed the best."

The janitor stood nearby in humility, awe and fear. If the CEO that he had followed for so long could receive no commendation from the Lord, what could he expect? His eyes were cast down and tears touched his cheeks when Jesus put His hands on the janitor's shoulders and said, "Son, lift your eyes." The janitor did and looked into the face of the Lord he loved.

The smile on Jesus' face caused a thrill to leap through his heart and in astonishment he heard Jesus say, "Turn around, son, and tell me what you see."

With the Lord's strong arm around his shoulders, the janitor turned and to his wonder he saw acres of people coming toward him. Their expressions reflected pure love and joy such as he had never known.

He turned to Jesus and said, "Lord, I recognize only a few. Who are the others?"

Jesus said, "Those you recognize are the ones you told of My love and the others are those they told. They are here now to thank you. Enter into the joy prepared for you from the...."

As Jesus said "foundations of the world," the joyful reunion was made complete. The angels sang, "Glory to God and to the Lamb." And the celebration that is eternal was joined.

You see, both men had opportunities, just like you and I. One built a fortune here, and the other there. One was temporary, one eternal. Both were the result of choices. Which type of fortune are you choosing?

That's the vision - light shining into the darkness of the marketplace through companies run by men and women gripped by the eternal perspective. They are seeing beyond today into forever, realizing that what we have been given is not for ourselves, but for service to the King of Kings. They are letting Him direct its use. He is the light of the world. Let Him shine.

Appendix A

COUNCIL OF ADVISORS

The Book of Proverbs contains at least 24 references to the value of godly counsel. Over and over again it calls our attention to the need to listen to God speak through others and the foolishness of unneccessarily standing alone.

Many have found great help in the formation and ongoing operation of a "Council of Advisors." Basically, such a council is a group of like-minded, spiritually mature believers, with relevant experience and perspective, who meet with you regularly, pray with/for you, and give you counsel and advice. The number can be as little as you and one other, but ideally there will be three or more (Ecclesiastes 4:12). Tremendous spiritual synergism takes place when two or more gather together to seek the mind of the Lord.

Many have found great advantage in forming a group of four to six to provide counsel and accountability to one another. Others find that a small group of one or two others who meet solely to pray and counsel them is more suitable.

Where C12 Groups exist they provide an excellent custom designed resource for this purpose. These groups consist of 10-15 Christian business Owners and CEOs and are facilitated by professional C12 Area Chairs. Membership is by invitation only and there is a monthly fee for membership.

Forming a Council of Advisors begins with prayer. Ask God to give you the names of people who could be wise advisors for you. Write down the names that come to mind. Look for those for whom you have spiritual respect. Don't prejudge whom He might provide. A good mix of spiritual maturity, business skill and experience might be ideal. After you have your list, begin to visit them one-by-one and ask each person. Explain your purpose and then ask them to pray about participating for your mutual benefit.

If you have questions contact
The C12 Group ®
www.c12group.com

Appendix B

A Strategic Plan for Ministry

C12's "Strategic Plan" material is a guide designed to help you utilize the basic process flow used in developing a business plan. That is, its workbook layout is designed to analyze potential, identify purpose, explore possibilities and resources, and craft a plan to take specific action. These are the steps of any good business plan, and this same conceptual thinking should be employed in planning ministry through a business.

A Strategic Plan for Ministry is simple to use, applicable to businesses of any size, and proven to be very successful in helping to launch or expand the process and practices of companies engaging in marketplace ministry. By using familiar methods and thought processes, it moves the idea of ministry in and through a business committed to Christ from the philosophical or theological to the practical and "do-able."

A copy of *A Strategic Plan for Ministry* can be obtained from The C12 Group® online store at www.C12Group.com.

C12 GUIDING PRINCIPLES

MISSION   To change the world by bringing forth the Kingdom of God in the marketplace through the companies and lives of those He calls to run businesses for Him.

VISION   To see an active global Christian CEO/Owner network with C12 groups in every community of 50,000 or more.

DOCTRINE   Simply, Jesus Christ is Lord, the whole Bible is wholly true, God has an eternal plan for each believer's life and that plan includes their business.

PROMISE   To be an example of all we promote and to be accountable to our members seeking their correction when any deviation may appear. We serve as a resource for education, encouragement, challenge, inspiration, and accountability.

C12 groups meet monthly across America and are impacting business owners, their employees, customers, suppliers, and competitors for Christ. Christian business owners and CEOs are learning the significance of leading thriving companies as platforms for ministry, and discovering eternal as well as temporal benefits, as they "build great businesses for a greater purpose."

If you are a Christian business Owner or CEO and are interested in learning more about becoming a C12 member, or possibly starting a group in your area, please visit our website or contact us directly.

The C12 Group, LLC
4101 Piedmont Parkway
Greensboro, NC 27410
336-841-7100
www.C12Group.com